CYNDI LAUPER

by CHRIS CROCKER

WANDERER BOOKS
Published by Simon & Schuster, Inc. • New York

THANKS TO JENNIFER GILBERT
FOR TECHNICAL ASSISTANCE

SPECIAL THANKS TO GLENN MORROW

Picture Credits: Laurie Paladino, title page, pgs. 23, 39, 42, 53, 56 (bottom); John Bellissimo, pgs. 8, 16, 30, 33, 56 (top); Robin Kaplan/ Retna Ltd., pg. 13; Laura Levine, p. 19; Ebet Roberts Photography, pgs. 25, 44; Gary Gershoff, pgs. 35, 61; David Seelig/Star File, pg. 50; Larry Busacca, pg. 51; Chuck Pulin/Star File, pg. 58.

Photo Research: Amanda Rubin

Published by WANDERER BOOKS
A Division of Simon & Schuster, Inc.
Simon & Schuster Building
1230 Avenue of the Americas
New York, New York 10020

Designed by Irving Perkins Associates
Manufactured in the United States of America
10 9 8 7 6 5 4 3 2 1

Also available in Julian Messner Library Edition.

Library of Congress Cataloging in Publication Data

Crocker, Chris.
  Cyndi Lauper.

  Discography: p.
  Summary: A brief biography highlighting the career
of the popular rock singer.
    1. Lauper, Cyndi,—Juvenile literature.
2. Rock musicians—United States—Biography—Juvenile
literature. [1. Lauper, Cyndi. 2. Singers.
3. Rock music] I. Title.
ML3930.L18C7   1985   784.5′4′00924   [B] [92]   84-27084
ISBN 0-671-55478-6 (lib. bdg.)
ISBN 0-671-55475-1 (pbk.)

CONTENTS

DO YOU KNOW THIS GIRL?   7

CYNDI'S ROOTS   10

SELF-SUFFICIENT CYNDI   15

ON STAGE   18

BLUE ANGEL   22

A NEW BEGINNING   29

SHE'S SO UNUSUAL   32

SWEET SUCCESS   38

VIDEO MANIA   41

FASHION SENSE—OR NON-SENSE   46

CYNDI VS. CAPTAIN LOU   52

CYNDI ON THE TUBE   55

A LOOK AT THE FUTURE   60

DISCOGRAPHY   62

CYNDI'S FAN CLUB   63

ABOUT THE AUTHOR   63

DO YOU KNOW THIS GIRL?

Her name is Cyndi Lauper. Maybe you know her as the one who sings "Girls Just Want to Have Fun." Maybe you know her as the star of some of the zaniest rock videos ever created, or for her lopsided yellow-orange hairdo and the wildest outfits that anybody ever dared to wear in public. Maybe you know all about Cyndi Lauper. Or do you?

Would you believe it if somebody told you that Cyndi Lauper:

- worked as a geisha girl in a restaurant for a Japanese businessman
- was once sued for $80,000 by her own manager
- lived alone in the Canadian wilderness with only her dog to keep her company
- doesn't drive because she's too worried that she'll run somebody over
- used to perform as a Janis Joplin imitator
- marched in peace rallies protesting the Vietnam War
- was once an opening act for the punk group The Ramones
- spoke in ancient Babylonian on coast-to-coast live television
- has sung before adoring fans as far away as Australia and Japan
- sells an album every fifteen seconds.

Cyndi Lauper

Well, it's all true. The *real* story of Cyndi Lauper is every bit as wild and wacky as one of her music videos. It's the story of a girl who tackled a lifetime of setbacks and disappointments to become an international pop sensation. And once you've read about her, you'll agree that there's nobody sharper, nobody flashier, nobody gutsier, and nobody *nutsier* than Cyndi Lauper!

CYNDI'S ROOTS

On June 22, 1953, the summer solstice, the sun shone longer than any other day that year.

Well, June 22, 1953 was certainly the longest day of the year for a certain Mr. and Mrs. Lauper of Brooklyn, New York. It was the day that their baby was born—a perfect baby girl who started screaming at the top of her lungs as soon as she came into the world. Her name was Cynthia Lauper.

Things didn't run too smoothly for Cyndi's big entrance into the world. As Cyndi once said, she was "almost born in a taxicab, on the way to Boulevard Hospital in Queens."

Cyndi's first home was in Brooklyn, one of the boroughs that make up New York City. She grew up in a section called Williamsburg. Although it's a part of New York City, Williamsburg is miles away from New York's bright lights and skyscrapers, and is a lot like any other quiet town in America.

Cyndi grew up with her sister Elen and her brother Butch. Their father was a shipping clerk and an amateur xylophonist whom their mother divorced when Cyndi was five years old. Cyndi's mom then took the children and moved to an area in Queens—also a borough of New York City—called Ozone Park.

Ozone Park is another quiet section like Williamsburg, except it was even quieter and farther from the excitement of New York. Cyndi has remarked on how far she felt from the real world in Ozone Park, but the boredom of growing up there may have brought about a positive change in her life.

At the age of five, little Cynthia Lauper was singing. She's always liked to sing, as she once told *New York* magazine: "I always sang—I sang before I talked. When I was sad, I'd sing and I'd feel better."

Cyndi would sing for the older people in the neighborhood—of course, when you're five almost *everybody* in your neighborhood is older than you. She loved to sing songs from the Broadway musicals that were so popular in the 1950s, and from which many of the biggest hits of the day came. She sang songs by the famous songwriters Rodgers and Hammerstein, who wrote some of the best-loved musicals of all time.

Cyndi's favorite Rodgers and Hammerstein show was *South Pacific* which took place on a tropical island. For the neighbors, she would sing "Bali Ha'i" and "Happy Talk," from that musical. Some of the neighbors may have liked her singing, but Cyndi seems to remember things a little differently.

Just what did Cyndi's neighbors think of her musical talent? This is what she told *Rock Fever*: "'She's not going to sing again, is she? Why can't she just *listen* to music for a change?' They were hopeful that I'd give it up, but I never did."

Cyndi was constantly exposed to music as she grew up. Her mother would play records by singers like Mario Lanza, who made women swoon with his big hit "Be My Love." She would also play records by Broadway star Ethel Merman, who was known for belting out her theme song, "There's No Business Like Show Business." And singers like the Boswell Sisters, Eileen Farrell, and Fanny Brice were also often heard in Cyndi's household.

In the early '60s, Barbra Streisand became a favorite. Streisand had made a big splash at that time because of her powerful voice and her comic acting talent. She starred in the movie *Funny Girl,* a musical based on the life of Fanny Brice, a star in the '20s who was famous for her strong voice and clowning around, so it was a perfect role for Barbra Streisand. Many people have compared Cyndi Lauper to both Barbra Streisand *and* Fanny Brice. Although their similarities are easy to see, Cyndi may end up being the zaniest of them all!

Another kind of music Cyndi listened to as a young girl was jazz. Jazz is said to be the only truly American art form and it's a lot more complicated than popular music.

Cyndi's mom played records by such jazz singers as Billie Holiday and Ella Fitzgerald. These singers made their voices sigh or wail to the music. Sometimes they sang nonsense syllables—what is called scat singing. Ella Fitzgerald was especially good at singing things like "skweedle-de-ah-dop-ah-doodle-de-zah!"

Cyndi would listen to the jazz singers and imitate their voices. Learning the tricky rules of jazz wasn't easy for a little girl, but it would come to benefit Cyndi in later years.

One of Cyndi's favorite jazzmen was Louis "Satchmo" Armstrong. One of the greatest jazz musicians who ever lived, today the U.S. government actually mints gold medallions with his picture on them. Satchmo made his reputation as a trumpet player, but later in his career he became a singer. Well, sort of. Louis Armstrong had a voice so low and raspy that he sounded like a bullfrog. He croaked out his songs. Cyndi still likes to imitate Satchmo and you might occasionally hear her singing his song "All That Meat and No Potatoes." She sings it in the same bouncy, bullfrog voice.

Mrs. Lauper was happy that Cyndi was a creative girl. She encouraged Cyndi to use her imagination and stretch her abilities. Still, as in any other family, Cyndi and her mom would fight, leaving the mother at a complete loss about what to do with the daughter. She would pray to St. Jude for Cyndi. (In the Catholic Church, St. Jude is the

Cyndi and mom

patron saint of desperate cases.) It seems that some of those prayers may have worked since, as a teenager, Cyndi was involved in a few car accidents, and miraculously was never seriously injured.

She also joined in peace marches protesting the war in Vietnam. The '60s were an emotional time and sometimes antiwar rallies erupted into violence.

Cyndi's mom thought it would be better for Cyndi to go to boarding school, so she was sent to a convent school in upstate New York. The school was run by nuns who could never see eye-to-eye with Cyndi Lauper. Is that hard to believe? Cyndi was never going to end up wearing the same black-and-white outfit every day!

After six long months at the convent school, Cyndi was expelled. She and the nuns had had their final argument, and she was back in Ozone Park.

Cyndi's high school years were more like a war *against* high school, because she was never very happy at any of the high schools she attended. She went to four different high schools and she never graduated from one! But she wasn't going to be beaten by the high school system. Cyndi went to the state of New York and was granted a general equivalency diploma. She had won the war against high school, but there were bigger challenges that she wanted to face. Cyndi would soon leave home.

SELF-SUFFICIENT CYNDI

At the age of 17, Cyndi Lauper moved away from Ozone Park. She was going to be alone in the great, wide world. Well, *almost* alone. Cyndi brought her family dog along, a mutt named Sparkle. Little did Sparkle know that Cyndi would someday make him a rock video star!

The first place Cyndi moved to was Long Island, not far from her home borough of Queens. But Long Island was too much like Ozone Park. She needed a complete change of scenery, and that's exactly what she got!

Cyndi packed Sparkle and her belongings up and moved to the Canadian woods. Canada has many beautiful forests, and Cyndi lived in a heavily wooded area in the province of Ontario. She lived alone in the isolated Canadian wilderness with only a tent for shelter and Sparkle to defend her. After a couple of weeks alone, Cyndi began to miss other people.

Cyndi moved back over the United States border and into the snowy state of Vermont, which attracts thousands of skiers every winter. It was near Stowe, the biggest skiing resort on the East Coast, that Cyndi and Sparkle stayed.

She attended a nearby art college and became interested in the great painters. One of her favorites was Vincent Van Gogh.

It wasn't always easy fitting in at school.

Van Gogh was a genius who had lived a lonely life. Hardly anyone appreciated his moody landscapes until after he had died. Cyndi always felt she could identify with him. He had trouble fitting in, just like she had, and her appreciation for the art of Van Gogh is something that she has kept with her.

To help defray the costs of school, Cyndi made extra money by taking odd jobs. Most odd jobs are pretty boring, but with Cyndi Lauper on the payroll, the jobs probably became a lot *odder* than they started out! She worked as a waitress and as a model for painting classes.

Cyndi still had problems with school and she found herself fighting against its restrictions, just as she had in Queens. Cyndi once described what things were like for her at college: "I liked to wear bright clothes and roller skates when it wasn't fashionable. I didn't get along with the teachers, who saw me as stupid when I was being creative."

When Cyndi couldn't stand it anymore, she and Sparkle headed back to Ozone Park. She talked about those depressing days in *Rolling Stone*: "I used to walk and walk and walk. I felt like I was going to walk off the end of the earth."

No matter how sad she was, Cyndi still needed to work. She worked as a secretary and sold stockings in a shoe store. She even had a job piercing people's ears! She tried to put her gift of gab to work and sold judo and karate lessons over the telephone. Although she made a furious pitch to sell those martial arts lessons, she admits today that she didn't know a thing about judo or karate.

One of Cyndi's last odd jobs was as a "hot walker" at the Belmont Park racetrack. Horses are such big animals that when they get worked up in a horserace, it takes a while to calm them down. Cyndi's job was to walk the horses around until they cooled down after a workout. As much fun as it might have been to work with these beautiful animals, she knew what her true calling was.

Cyndi Lauper had to become a rock-'n'-roller.

ON STAGE

There was one thing that started Cyndi Lauper on her career in music: the guitar given to her by her sister Elen. Cyndi started learning songs on the guitar as soon as she got it. The first song she learned was "Greensleeves," an English folksong that is hundreds of years old.

In the early and mid 1960s, folk music became extremely popular. Singers like Bob Dylan, Joan Baez, and Peter, Paul and Mary made Cyndi want to get involved in folk-singing. She played her guitar in the park or at hootenannys—a kind of folk music party.

She also liked Grace Slick, lead singer in the Jefferson Airplane. Although they would eventually become the rock group Jefferson Starship, the Jefferson Airplane started out as a folk group.

That was a pattern that developed in rock-'n'-roll in the late '60s. Folk music was being replaced with folk-rock and more turbulent styles of rock-'n'-roll. Cyndi's music reflected this pattern; she was growing away from the soft acoustic guitars of folk and loved the beat of rock-'n'-roll.

She has been a fan of such rock-'n'-rollers as Little Eva who, despite her name, had a big voice and a big hit with the song "Loco-motion." Cyndi was also fond of early rock stars like Eddie Cochran, Frankie Lymon, and Brenda Lee.

Of all the rock-'n'-roll groups, Cyndi's favorite was the Beatles. She and her sister would do the dinner dishes at night and sing Beatles songs. She was fascinated by the way John Lennon's voice harmonized with Paul McCartney's. When she sang with Elen, Cyndi tried to

18

duplicate those harmonizations. Trying to match the Beatles' classic vocals was often frustrating for her, but the practice would prove to be good for her.

In 1974, Cyndi Lauper started singing professionally.

At first, it wasn't easy for her to find work. She sang on street corners in Greenwich Village for a while. Anybody strolling by could have seen a free Cyndi Lauper concert—provided they were on the right sidewalk. Of course, more people thought of Cyndi as a crazy person than as a future rock-'n'-roll star.

At long last Cyndi was hired to sing with a rock-'n'-roll band called Doc West. She was a backup singer—a singer who harmonized with the lead singer. On stage, backup singers are never the center of attention. Often, the role of a backup singer is to look pretty and sway her hips. Not much of a job! In addition to singing for Doc West, Cyndi was expected to *dance* as well, but since this was her first *paying* music job, she thought it wiser not to complain.

Cyndi onstage—a far cry from singing in the street.

Groups like Doc West that only play hits by others are called cover bands or copy bands. The audiences that the group played to were mostly rock fans who wanted to hear the hits that other rock bands had made famous. Doc West gave their audience what they wanted.

Doc West played disco as well as rock-'n'-roll. Cyndi sang songs that had been hits by Patti Labelle or Chaka Khan. Still, doing songs like "I've Got the Music in Me" night after night was good practice for her. "That was also when I first discovered that I had some harmonics in my voice," Cyndi said recently. "They're kind of like whistle notes."

Doc West put Cyndi's vocal talents to use in a way she never dreamed. She impersonated Janis Joplin!

Janis Joplin was a rock-'n'-roll singer who died tragically in the late 1960s. Since Janis had so many fans, some groups imitated her as a tribute. Cyndi's job was to *become* Janis Joplin. She sang like Janis and dressed like Janis. People would come up to Cyndi after her show and tell her how much she reminded them of Janis Joplin. Her Joplin imitation was a big hit. There was just one problem: it was driving Cyndi crazy!

She knew she had the talent to make it as a solo performer. She knew that rock-'n'-roll fans would love her nutty personality. But how would anyone ever get to know the real Cyndi Lauper if she had to turn into Janis Joplin every night? It didn't take her long to make up her mind. Cyndi stopped singing for Doc West.

The next group she got involved with was called Flyer. Working with Flyer wasn't a great improvement over Doc West. Flyer, like Doc West, was another cover band. Cyndi was through imitating Janis Joplin, but she still had to sing the same types of songs. "Singing other people's songs didn't sit well with my creative process," Cyndi once remarked to *New York* magazine.

Singing in a cover band may have stifled Cyndi's imagination, but she had no idea of the type of trouble she was about to run into. Cyndi Lauper was losing her voice, and in 1977, she had to leave Flyer. She could scarcely sing at all.

The human voice is like a musical instrument, and there's a right and a wrong way to play it. For years, Cyndi had been singing the wrong way. Even though she sounded fine she was damaging her voice a little bit every time she sang. Classically trained singers are very careful to sing the proper way, but rock-'n'-roll singers almost never teach themselves how to sing. They can be ruining their voices and never know it.

Now it was happening to Cyndi Lauper. She wasn't sure she'd ever sing again.

The friend who took her place in Flyer recommended that Cyndi see a voice teacher named Katie Agresta. Cyndi agreed to meet with her. It was her only chance.

Katie Agresta explained to Cyndi what she had been doing to her voice over the years. Although she had done extensive damage to her vocal cords, they weren't completely destroyed. Cyndi needed to learn how a classical vocalist takes care of her voice. Under Katie's care, Cyndi embarked on a program that stressed correct breathing techniques and other "tricks of the trade" that give opera singers their powerful voices.

Katie Agresta has helped quite a few rock-'n'-roll singers over the years. One of her other students was Dee Snider, the lead singer for the heavy-metal band Twisted Sister. Between Cyndi Lauper and Dee Snider, Katie Agresta must've had the weirdest-dressed students of any voice teacher in the world!

Of course, Cyndi's vocal cords *did* return to their old vitality. But it took a full year of vocal therapy with Katie Agresta before Cyndi was ready to sing in public again.

This time there would be no more cover bands and no more tributes to *other* rock stars. Cyndi was determined to make it on her own.

BLUE ANGEL

Cyndi Lauper had a fresh approach to music, thanks to her recent vocal training, and she was anxious to show everyone what she'd learned.

Her first appearance after her vocal cords had healed was in Greenwich Village. After years of performing (or "gigging") around Long Island, she was finally playing in the heart of New York. Cyndi's debut was at Trude Heller's, an elegant nightspot on the west side of Greenwich Village.

Cyndi was playing solo so she had no choice but to let her slightly silly personality shine through. When she did, people loved her. One night, a man named Ted Rosenblatt sat in the audience watching Cyndi sing. He met her later and offered to become her manager. Knowing how important it is for a rock musician to have a good manager, she agreed to their partnership.

Most of the time, a manager allows rock-'n'-roll musicians to devote themselves to their music by handling the business affairs of his or her client. The manager makes sure that a rock musician or band plays enough gigs to make money, and works to get a recording contract for the musician. Making records is absolutely crucial to a rock-'n'-roller's career. Of course, the manager *wants* the musician to make a lot of money. If the client gets rich, the manager gets rich as well.

Now Cyndi had a manager, but no band to back her up. That's where Ted Rosenblatt came in. He introduced her to a man named John Turi, who played piano and saxophone and, like Ted Rosenblatt, he enjoyed Cyndi's act at Trude Heller's. For John, Cyndi was the vocalist he'd been looking for and before long, he asked her to start a rock band with him. This was too good an offer to pass up.

They called the group Blue Angel, and it featured Cyndi on lead vocals, John on piano and saxophone, Arthur "Rockin A" Neilson on guitar, Lee Brovitz on bass, and Johnny "Bullet" Morelli on drums. Cyndi and John wrote the songs as well.

Blue Angel gigged most of the New York nightclubs for a year or so. Cyndi was finally singing in New York, but more important, she was singing her *own* songs.

"People have always said I couldn't sing, always tried to label me," Cyndi once told *Rolling Stone*. "I ain't worried about them, because the minute I open my mouth

"I can blow them right offa their chairs."

and sing, I can blow them right offa their chairs. They can't take your talent away from ya."

And true to her word, Cyndi was blowing rock-'n'-roll clubgoers right offa their chairs alright. Some of the people Cyndi impressed were music critics. A music critic is someone who writes about music for a newspaper or magazine, and it's his or her job to tell the reader who's good and who's bad in music. Well, the music critics were in agreement about Cyndi Lauper. She was great! But, although their verdict on Cyndi was unanimous, their verdict on the *rest* of Blue Angel, unfortunately, wasn't so positive. They thought Cyndi would have been better off without them.

Cyndi wouldn't think of leaving Blue Angel, however.

One night, at an uptown nightclub called Trax, she met another man who would change her musical career: Steve Massarsky. He'd seen Cyndi on stage and thought she was fabulous. This was a little hard for her to believe, since she was not at her best the night he saw her. Cyndi had been bumping into the band's equipment as she sang. She even tripped over the other guys on the bandstand.

None of this mattered to Steve Massarsky, who immediately offered to become Blue Angel's new manager. It seemed like a good idea for Cyndi and the band and before long, he was in charge.

One of the first big changes that Steve brought to Blue Angel was an obvious improvement. He got them gigs in larger clubs and even concert halls. More and more people could see Cyndi and Blue Angel. Their popularity was on the rise.

Steve also had Blue Angel warming up for better-known groups. When a group goes on first it "warms up" the audience for the bigger-name band. It's one of the ways a group gets wider exposure. Blue Angel warmed up for such diverse rock acts as Steve Forbert and Joe Jackson. They even warmed up for The Ramones!

Blue Angel

The biggest break for Cyndi and Blue Angel was still to come. In late 1979, Blue Angel signed a recording contract with Polydor Records. A contract with a major record company like Polydor is a rock-'n'-roll band's dream.

Still, Blue Angel's dream didn't come true without a bit of a fight. Like so many music critics, Polydor had liked Cyndi a lot more than they liked the rest of the group. They encouraged Cyndi to get rid of Blue Angel. Cyndi was steadfast, though. If Blue Angel went, she went. After a six month battle of wills, Cyndi won. Blue Angel was going to make its first record!

The album was simply titled *Blue Angel*. It was the first chance people had to listen to Cyndi Lauper on their record players, and it gave people a good idea of the kind of music the band made.

Blue Angel was a group that tried to capture the sounds of rock-'n'-roll of the 1950s and early 1960s. Bands like this are sometimes called revival bands because they revive old styles of rock that people don't hear much anymore.

Blue Angel tried to capture the spirit of some of the rock stars that Cyndi listened to when she was growing up. On *Blue Angel,* Cyndi made all her musical memories come out in her singing.

One of the most interesting songs on *Blue Angel* is called "I Had a Love." It's a very dramatic song which starts out with pounding percussion and the click of castanets. Cyndi's voice sounds weak and whiny at first but, as the song progresses, her vocals take on the powerful qualities of Little Eva or even Grace Slick.

The soulful side of Cyndi Lauper is revealed on "Anna Blue." Her voice is frail and helpless in this song. It's about a very lonely girl, and since it's a blues song, the name "Anna Blue" is fitting.

Blues is a style of music that is usually very slow and mournful. Traditionally, blues songs express the pain and frustration of the person who sings them. Over the years, musicians have written blues songs about anything sad. In "Anna Blue," John Turi plays a snaky solo on his saxophone. When Cyndi sings, her voice becomes a wail. If you hear singers wailing or shrieking in rock-'n'-roll groups, you're hearing the influence of the blues.

Rockabilly was another style that Blue Angel was famous for. The original rockabilly musicians took two different kinds of music and blended them together: rock-'n'-roll and hillbilly music. Usually played at fast tempos, rockabilly singers sometimes cram as many words into a song as they possibly can. Sometimes they hoot and holler. When Cyndi was a girl, Elvis Presley and Eddie Cochran were the rockabilly stars. Today, revival groups like the Stray Cats play rockabilly music.

In the Blue Angel song "Late," Cyndi starts things off in classic rockabilly style. The saxophone honks along with Cyndi in "Late" as she makes the kind of hoots you'd hear on a rockabilly record. To make the picture complete, Arthur Neilson gives his guitar the twangy sound of music of the 1950s. All in all, *Blue Angel* is a fun record to listen to.

Cyndi wasn't very happy with how the album *looked,* though. On the front cover, she is wearing dark pedal pushers and polka dotted bobby socks. With her mouth wrinkled up and her eyes all squinty, it's the kind of goony pose you'd expect from Cyndi Lauper. Still, she thought the cover was poorly designed. She even thought the picture of her made her look like Big Bird!

On the back cover, Cyndi is wearing a banana-yellow party dress with a beautiful floral pattern embroidered on the bodice. There is one other thing you might notice: she looks extremely uncomfortable.

Cyndi wasn't having any fun in Blue Angel at this time. Things just weren't going right. Once, to create publicity for Blue Angel, they sponsored a "Win a Date with Cyndi Lauper" contest. When Cyndi went out to dinner with the winner of the contest, she accidentally spit some of her half-chewed food into his lap! It was a date he'd *never* forget!

At that point, Blue Angel wasn't even making enough money for Cyndi to support herself. To help make ends meet, she started working in a clothing store called Screaming Mimi's. Her boss at the time, Biff Chandler, remembers that Cyndi was going through a difficult period, but "she pretty much kept all that to herself. We knew she was having problems, but she always had the most wonderful personality. She never let the problems bother her, they never affected her work. She was always a total delight."

Cyndi was looking for odd jobs—something she hoped she'd never have to return to. "When I started singing, everything came," Cyndi once remarked. "Before I started singing I was always fired from jobs because I didn't fit in. I dressed too funny . . . I did odd jobs. *Really* odd jobs. I was an American geisha girl in a Japanese restaurant where I would sing and sell drinks. I got the job not because I was a good waitress, but because I could sing."

The restaurant, located on New York's Upper East Side

was called Miho. Most of the customers were Japanese businessmen who missed the kind of entertainment they'd see back home. Years after she'd stopped imitating Janis Joplin, Cyndi Lauper was imitating a Japanese geisha girl!

But things were going to get much worse for Cyndi.

Polydor Records decided not to let Blue Angel make another record. The band, angry and disappointed over losing their recording contract, fired their manager, Steve Massarsky.

He responded by taking Blue Angel to court—and suing them for $80,000.

In court, it was determined that Cyndi could never pay the money Steve was asking for. She was declared legally bankrupt by a New York judge. This was the only way she could avoid paying her former manager. At the age of 29, Cyndi Lauper was penniless.

A NEW BEGINNING

December 7, 1981 was the fortieth anniversary of the bombing of Pearl Harbor. It was also the day that Cyndi Lauper met a lanky man by the name of David Wolff. Cyndi and Dave took an immediate liking to each other.

Dave Wolff was about 32 when he met Cyndi. He, just like Cyndi, had worked his share of odd jobs; he had been a messenger and even worked as an exterminator for a while. Dave had gone to Babson College as a business student, and was now sharpening his talents as a rock-'n'-roll manager.

Dave already managed a couple of groups, including the Major Thinkers, a snappy dance band that played in many of New York's smaller clubs. He also managed a group called ArcAngel. Both ArcAngel and the Major Thinkers recorded for Portrait Records, which is part of CBS Records, one of the biggest record companies in the world.

Cyndi and Dave became personally involved as the months progressed, and when Cyndi was finally free of her old manager, Dave Wolff took over from him. She had finally found a manager she could rely on.

Cyndi soon signed a contract with Portrait Records. They promised her freedom that she had never had at Polydor. "Record companies didn't want creativity," Cyndi once remarked to the *New York Sunday News,*

29

With a new manager and recording contract, Cyndi faced a new be
ginning.

"they wanted safe clones. But this company let me do songs that said what I wanted to say."

The man who produced Cyndi's first real solo album was Rick Chertoff, who had previously produced a record for Joe Piscopo of "Saturday Night Live."

Rick Chertoff and Cyndi set about the difficult task of choosing songs for her to sing on the album. Originally Cyndi planned to use only other peoples' songs on her record, but it wouldn't be like her old days in those Long Island cover bands. Cyndi wasn't picking songs according to their popularity, she was picking songs that she *liked*.

Yet, no matter how much Cyndi enjoyed the "cover" songs planned for the album, she felt she had to write some new material as well. "I decided to just go ahead and do it," she recalls, "though I hadn't written many new songs. I had broken up my partnership with John Turi, and didn't like the idea of just singing other peoples' songs. But, for *She's So Unusual,* producer Rick Chertoff and I selected songs that enabled me to keep my integrity and that meant something to me. And I wrote some, too."

There were really only three musicians who played on *She's So Unusual.* Along with Cyndi, on both lead and backup vocals, are Eric Bazilian on guitar, bass and a few other instruments, and Rob Hyman playing keyboards. (A keyboard can be an organ, synthesizer, or anything played like a piano.)

Cyndi, Eric, and Rob recorded the album almost entirely by themselves. In a recording studio, you can record instruments one at a time. You never need to get a band together—they can be assembled on a tape a lot more easily. There were about ten other musicians who played or sang on the album, but their contributions were a lot less important.

By the fall of 1983, Cyndi was ready to assault the world. But was the world ready for its first undiluted dose of Cyndi Lauper? Nobody knew. . . .

She's So Unusual was released on October 14, 1983.

SHE'S SO UNUSUAL

MONEY CHANGES EVERYTHING

Cyndi's first solo album starts off with a steady dance beat as the synthesizer plays a soaring, buzzing theme. "Money Changes Everything" was originally recorded by a group called the Brains. It's a biting song about how people can let money ruin their relationships.

Cyndi may have been saying something else when she chose "Money Changes Everything" to be her opening song. She could have used the song to comment on her need for a record company that would allow her to make a well-produced record. *Blue Angel* could have been a bigger hit if it had been better made, but the recording quality was very flat and dull. On *She's So Unusual*, the music sounds three-dimensional.

Cyndi wanted her record to sound perfect, and she knew how expensive it is to make a perfect-sounding record. Now with the backing of her new record company, she could pay for one.

GIRLS JUST WANT TO HAVE FUN

"Girls Just Want to Have Fun" has already become Cyndi Lauper's theme song. It starts with a loony effect that sounds like a spring unwinding. Accompanied by bouncing guitars and synthesizers, Cyndi's voice rings out like a

She's so unusual."

bell. At times, her singing is so deep and strong you can really hear the classical training in her voice.

"Girls Just Want to Have Fun" was written by Robert Hazard. Cyndi loved the tune, but she didn't like the song's lyrics, so she changed them. On the dust jacket of the album, Cyndi thanks Robert Hazard, adding "(for letting me change your song)."

Cyndi feels very strong about the message the song conveys. Cyndi told *Rock Fever*: "When I was a kid, Christmas and Easter holidays weren't much fun for me because I used to be cleaning with Mom. Setting the table and wiping dishes while my brother was out playing. I *did* just want to have fun. Ideas like 'girls just want to have fun' can really touch other young girls, which is what I wanted to do. Touch humanity and communicate. Boy am I deep!"

WHEN YOU WERE MINE

Rock superstar Prince wrote "When You Were Mine," a song about liking somebody better after you've broken up with them. It describes a confusing situation, but Prince's songs often involve mixed emotions.

The sounds of the synthesizers in "When You Were Mine" are also mixed. While sometimes sounding like trumpets, they sound like whirring electronic toys in other parts of the song.

TIME AFTER TIME

Side One ends with Cyndi's saddest song, "Time after Time," a song about separation, loneliness, and possible reunion.

The drum beats click like the ticking of a wall clock. A guitar is picked very slowly and thoughtfully. When Cyndi sings, her lonely voice echoes a little. In the chorus, Cyndi's voice is joined by a man's voice which gives the song an air of romance. Many consider this to be Cyndi's finest.

Sometimes, Cyndi sings sad songs, with themes like separation and loneliness.

SHE BOP

The craziest song on *She's So Unusual* has to be "She Bop." The synthesizers play a lurching melody that sounds like monster movie music. Cyndi uses all the hoots and pops from her rockabilly days. Still, there was another kind of singing that Cyndi may have used in "She Bop": scat singing. The silly nonsense words in "She Bop" sound like they could have been sung first by Ella Fitzgerald.

ALL THROUGH THE NIGHT

Cyndi Lauper's fourth single is "All through the Night." It starts with the synthesizer sounding like an electronic harp. Cyndi's voice, quiet and naive at first, is full of power in the finale.

"All through the Night" is a song about commitment between two people. It uses the image of a taxi meter that keeps on running, no matter what the cost.

WITNESS

This is the only song on the album that Cyndi cowrote with John Turi, her old partner from Blue Angel. Like some of the Blue Angel songs, "Witness" has an exotic atmosphere. The rattling of the drums makes it sound a little bit like reggae. This is probably the last Blue Angel song that anyone will ever hear.

I'LL KISS YOU

Bloopy synthesizers and a big angry drum beat start off in "I'll Kiss You." Cyndi sings her words with the same sort of rapidfire delivery that she used when she sang rockabilly songs. The big difference here is that Cyndi gives the stream of words a slightly punkier angle.

References to other rock-'n'-roll hits are made in the lyrics to "I'll Kiss You." "Last time she gave me Love Potion #8" is a line that refers to "Love Potion #9," the '50s Clovers hit that was also a hit for the Searchers in the '60s.

HE'S SO UNUSUAL

Cyndi may have been living out an old fantasy when she recorded "He's So Unusual." It was written in 1929 and Cyndi even sings the song in the kind of squeaky little voice that was popular in the '20s. Producer Rick Chertoff made the song sound scratchy and tinny, just as an old record would sound.

YEAH YEAH

"Yeah Yeah" is a lot like "She Bop." It's a song that doesn't mean very much but has a great dance beat. Cyndi and the chorus call back and forth to each other in a sing-along manner. "Yeah Yeah" is an appropriately zany way for *She's So Unusual* to end.

The cover of *She's So Unusual* features a photograph of Cyndi that makes her look frozen, like a painting. She's holding a tattered bouquet of flowers; her red dress and orange hair are in stark contrast to the cool blue bricks of the building behind her. Where did Cyndi find *blue* bricks, anyway?

On the back cover of the album, we see Cyndi from beneath the soles of her shoes. Painted on the soles is a section of *Starry Night* by Vincent Van Gogh whose moody paintings she still admires. Her shoes look like enchanted slippers, and from what happened to Cyndi's life after *She's So Unusual* was released, you'd think that she *was* wearing enchanted slippers!

SWEET SUCCESS

The success of *She's So Unusual* was astounding. It was just as Cyndi knew it would be. Give the people Cyndi Lauper and they'll be crying for more.

Cyndi thinks what made the album a hit was one simple thing. She was allowed to be herself. "I was really given my space on this album," she recalled. "With Rick and the musicians there was none of that feeling like, 'okay, let's do an album and get it out there.' It's dance music, it's experimental music, it's got warmth and humanity."

There was something else that Cyndi's album had— great songs. "Girls Just Want to Have Fun," "Time after Time," and "She Bop" have all been the most popular songs in the country. This may sound difficult to prove, but it's really very easy.

Record industry magazines like *Billboard* and *Cashbox* rate every song by how many copies of the single have been sold. Sometimes there are 100 places on a chart. Sometimes there are only 40. (This is where the expression "Top 40" comes from.) The better the public likes a record, the farther up the chart it goes. Every rock-'n'-roller wants his or her record to do well on the charts.

Well, on *Billboard*'s chart, "Girls Just Want to Have Fun" went to the #2 spot. There was only *one* song in the country that was more popular.

The same *Billboard* chart named "Time after Time"

he band. From left, Cyndi, Sandy Gennaro, John McCurry, John K.,
enni Hairston.

the national #1 single. Cyndi had achieved the dream of any rock musician, a #1 song.

Cyndi's success was still growing. Just one year after its release, *She's So Unusual* sold two million copies. The recording industry awards a platinum album to any artist who sells a million copies of his or her record. Cyndi's album was certified as double platinum.

How fast was Cyndi Lauper selling records? If she sold 2,000,000 albums in one year, how many did she sell every day?

Well, after doing some mathematical figuring, you would find that the result is approximately 5,480 albums a day. Take it a few steps further and you'd discover that one album was sold every fifteen seconds. Astounding!

Now that Cyndi was so popular, she began to do what she loves most: singing in front of live audiences. But, since Cyndi couldn't duplicate on stage what she could create in the studio, she had to hire a touring band.

Her new band was made up of John McCurry on guitar, Kenni Hairston on keyboards, John K on bass, and Sandy Gennaro on drums.

Toward the end of 1983 Cyndi had warmed up for the Kinks at New York's famous Roseland Ballroom. Only a few months later, she was the top act at the Ritz nightclub. She had finally become the main attraction.

Cyndi and her band toured all over the USA, from New York to California. She also played in Germany, Japan, and Australia. She was met by mobs of *Lauperites* all over the world. Why did people enjoy Cyndi wherever she went?

"I love people," Cyndi explained, "that's where the real rock-'n'-roll comes from—real people. That's why my songs work; because they're about real people."

VIDEO MANIA

If there was anyone left who hadn't heard Cyndi on the radio, they probably saw and heard her on TV. A new trend of the 1980s is for musicians to make videos of their songs, some of which look pretty much alike and become tiresome after the first viewing. Cyndi made sure that *nobody* would forget her videos!

In the same way that she hired Rick Chertoff to make her album sound great, she hired just the right people to make her videos look great, including a man named Edd Griles to direct them. He could make videos that were zany enough for Cyndi Lauper to enjoy. That was crucial. Above all she wanted her videos to be *funny*. "With my video I wanted to make people laugh," Cyndi said, "because humor is universal. That's part of being human."

GIRLS JUST WANT TO HAVE FUN

The video clip of "Girls Just Want to Have Fun" tells the story of one girl's battle with her parents. Cyndi plays the girl, as you'd guess, and Cyndi's mom plays—who else?—her mom. The role of Cyndi's father was played by professional wrestling manager Lou Albano.

Cyndi's mother sits and breaks eggs into a mixing bowl. That is, until Cyndi comes home later, which makes her mother crack an egg against her apron in despair. (Cyndi always tells people how proud she was of her mother— she could crack an egg in time with the music!)

Cyndi with mom in MTV video: "Girls Just Want to Have Fun."

Ignoring her father's warning, Cyndi calls up eight of her friends. No matter where they are or what they're doing, Cyndi's friends are all willing to chat.

At one point pictures of Cyndi and her pals turn into what looks like shiny round Christmas tree ornaments. Cyndi and company were squashed into those little balls by means of a sophisticated video computer called the Quantel Mirage. It handles some of the trickiest video effects ever seen.

Cyndi and her friends decide to make their own fun. They go on sort of a mini-parade through New York's Greenwich Village and Wall Street areas. As the girls dance towards Cyndi's house, more and more people get swept up in their wake.

By the time they return to her room, they have dozens of strangers with them. Finally, the overloaded bedroom spills people all over Cyndi's helpless parents. This ending was taken out of a Marx Brothers movie from the 1930s, but Cyndi makes it look like it's all hers.

"We danced all the way through Manhattan—it was fabulous," Cyndi told *New York* magazine. "To me, those girls reflected real life, and that's what I tried to portray, that kind of beauty."

The girls in the video really *were* Cyndi's friends. In addition to her mother, Cyndi's brother Butch and dog Sparkle appeared in the "Girls Just Want to Have Fun" video.

"My mother was wonderful," Cyndi joked with *Rolling Stone*. "Now it's gone to her head. She's picked out a stage name—Catrine Dominique—and she wears sunglasses whenever she walks Sparkle. As a matter of fact, Sparkle wears sunglasses now too."

TIME AFTER TIME

"Time after Time" is a very simple song; the video is much more complicated. It moves both backward and forward in time, and although it's easy to understand what's going on between the boy and girl in the video, we're never told exactly *why* these things are happening. "Time after Time" tells the story of how people can be pulled apart, even if they want to stay together.

Cyndi plays a girl who lives in a bullet-shaped Airstream trailer in the middle of the woods. She lives there with her boyfriend, who is played—no kidding!— by David Wolff, Cyndi's real-life boyfriend. The video even portrays how the two people in the video met years before.

Later in the video, Cyndi and her boyfriend get into a fight over her new orange hairdo with checkerboard shavings on the side. So disappointed by her boyfriend's reaction, she decides to move away.

The most touching scene in "Time After Time" comes when Cyndi has to say goodbye to her mother. Cyndi runs up to her and they hug each other on the front porch. As Cyndi runs back to the waiting car, Cyndi's mom puts her hand up to her mouth to stop a sudden sob. This scene becomes more moving when you think that there probably was a time when Cyndi had said goodbye to her mother in just this way. As the video ends, we see Cyndi

Cyndi with real-life boyfriend, David Wolff, in MTV video: "She Bop."

sitting in a departing train, wondering if she'll ever see her boyfriend again, a single tear running down her cheek.

"I try to be free and not have any inhibitions," Cyndi remarked to *People*. "My work is full of emotion. It's real, you can touch it."

SHE BOP

Cyndi's videos *were* very real. You knew Cyndi's friends and loved ones were in her videos—you could see them there. Maybe that's why Cyndi's third video, "She Bop," has nothing to do with reality at all. It's just one long fantasy in which every scene becomes even weirder than the one before it.

"She Bop" starts out in a giant, steamy take-out restaurant. David Wolff plays the mad fry cook at work in his bionic burger kitchen. A few minutes later, Dave becomes the leader of a motorcycle gang called the "Beefcake Charlys." He and Cyndi go on a wild road chase and they're both turned into cartoons!

It doesn't take more than a few seconds before Cyndi is back in human form. She stands before a police desk sergeant named the Big Bopper. Cyndi's mom and Lou Albano are in their bathrobes, obviously awakened after another one of Cyndi's midnight sprees.

Before anyone can make any sense of these scene, the police station dissolves and Cyndi is seen wearing a white tuxedo and top hat. This final scene was made in honor of the old Hollywood movies that Cyndi loved as a girl. (There were clips from vintage films in both of her previous videos, too.)

Dave appears dressed just like Cyndi, as if in a Fred Astaire musical. The two of them dance a bit of "the ol' soft shoe," and as the video draws to a close, Dave and Cyndi are seated on a glittery plywood man-in-the-moon. Giant, phony crescent moons are a Hollywood cliché of the first order. Only someone like Cyndi Lauper could get away with that!

FASHION SENSE—OR NON-SENSE

One of the most impressive things about Cyndi Lauper is her sense of fashion. Some people might say *nonsense* of fashion, but that probably wouldn't bother Cyndi a bit.

All her life, Cyndi has tried to look and dress the way *she* wanted, not just the way her friends did. She didn't try to look like a model or an actress, she only wanted to dress like Cyndi Lauper. It didn't matter if people thought she dressed a little weird.

Even when she was younger, she had a kooky look all her own. Instead of making Cyndi feel like an oddball, her freaky fashions would make her feel better. "When I looked at my clothes, I'd smile because it would cheer me up," Cyndi confided to *New York* magazine.

Cyndi's personal tastes in fashion led her to an antique clothing shop called Screaming Mimi's. When Blue Angel was making a lot of money, Cyndi shopped at Screaming Mimi's. When Blue Angel hit the skids, Cyndi started *working* at Screaming Mimi's!

Screaming Mimi's is an eccentric clothing store, to say the least. The ceiling and walls are painted pink with black trim. Paint is splattered all around—as though the whole room was an abstract painting.

The store is stocked with a variety of unusual fashions: tuxedos, tuxedo shirts, old ties, men's tweed overcoats, black evening dresses, vests, baggy trousers, socks, and classic hats.

Lots of celebrities shop at Screaming Mimi's. Actors and actresses from many of the most popular soap operas shop there, as have such well-known personalities as Diane Keaton and Roger Daltrey. Rock-'n'-rollers, including members of Jefferson Starship and Ratt, are said to stop by Screaming Mimi's when they're in New York. (There hasn't been any report of Boy George stopping at Screaming Mimi's. Nonetheless, Cyndi once told the *New York Sunday News* that she likes him, "though we're totally different. Have you ever seen him in a circle skirt?")

Screaming Mimi's is run by Biff Chandler, Laura Wills, and Connie Grunwald. Biff describes the shop this way: "We're definitely a cut above. Very selective, always try to reflect what's going on in current fashion. Just because we sell antique clothing doesn't mean we sell anything that's old. There are certain things we'd *never* buy. We don't sell women's coats. All our female customers want to dress in men's clothes. If they're getting dressed up to go out at night, then they want a black cocktail dress or a really outrageous party dress. A lot of our stuff has never been worn before. We have our own line of cosmetics, which Cyndi does use."

What would it have been like to walk into a clothing store and find Cyndi Lauper sitting behind the counter? "People really adored her because she was really entertaining to customers," said Laura Wills. "They would always come in and say, 'What an imaginative name, Screaming Mimi's'. We would not have to say a word; she would weave the most fantastic stories. She was really funny about who Screaming Mimi was—she was this woman; she lived in Hollywood. . . . She'd tell these really wild tales that were really fun."

For her boss, Biff Chandler, Cyndi was a model employee. "Well, I shouldn't say this," he once confided, "but she was the only employee I never yelled at. She was always totally delightful. Everybody thought she was crazy because she used to bring in her own tapes of the old '20s stars like Fanny Brice and Helen Kane."

Did working at Screaming Mimi's influence Cyndi's ideas about style? "I think so," Biff replied. "She definitely wanted to dress a certain way. Her own style. It took her a long time to figure out exactly what that was. She'd see all these people coming in, established musicians and other famous people. She'd see how they dressed and knew she wanted to dress her own way—definitely not like anybody else. There was always a series of questions: 'Is it too '50s?' 'Is it too punk?' 'Is it too much like this one?' 'Is it too much like that one?' "

Screaming Mimi's still has a certain amount of influence on Cyndi's wardrobe. Biff Chandler and Laura Wills are in charge of the outfits worn in Cyndi's videos. Laura concentrates on Cyndi's clothing and styling. Biff usually takes care of the other members of the cast. Laura also styled Cyndi for her photo session with Richard Avedon, the famous photographer.

What kind of clothes does Cyndi Lauper wear, anyway? Here's a short list of things that you might see Cyndi Lauper wearing:

a red crinoline dress
patterned white pedal
   pushers
a black cocktail dress
white fishnet stockings
green plastic sunglasses
plaid belts
a green taffeta dress
blue fishnet pattered stockings
plastic hoop earrings

black netting anklets
black netting fingerless
   gloves
a black straw boater
a fake pearl necklace
a green sleeveless satin
   blouse
pink tulle scarves
plaid elastic suspenders
metal chain bracelets
bullet belts

round-framed glasses
beaded ankle bracelets
metal studded belts
a frilly blue party dress
blue rhinestone bracelets
plastic clothespins
a denim jacket
black angora pompoms
a green brocade corset
a clustered red-beaded
    bracelet
a coiled-snake armlet
clear rhinestone earrings
pointy-framed sunglasses
black fishnet stockings
plastic chain belts
a black brocade corset
frilly petticoats

plastic chain bracelets
a leopard-skin headband
a white tuxedo jacket
a white prom dress
a plaid Ferrari cap
a strapless red lace long-
    line bra
argyle socks
rollerskates
leopard-skin pyjamas
blue elastic suspenders
chain anklets
a tropical print dress
a shag-fringed sleeveless
    top
a black wool shawl
brown and white two-tone
    shoes

Aside from clothes, Cyndi uses makeup in original ways as well. "She has her own makeup man and they work on her makeup together," said Biff Chandler. "She always tries to pick up somewhat. If she's wearing a blouse with flowers on it, she'll put flowers on her eyelids. Or polka dots. Or stripes."

"I'm not *trying* to be different," Cyndi told *Newsweek,* "I'm just saying it's okay to be yourself. And if you have a few quirky things, that's okay, too."

Should *you* try to dress like Cyndi Lauper? Actually, Cyndi wears so *many* different articles at a time, something you're wearing right now could've been part of a Cyndi Lauper outfit. Still, the last thing Cyndi would do is tell you what to wear.

What are Cyndi's feelings about this? "She really stresses individuality," says Biff Chandler. "She really hates to go out and see people looking like her. By dressing the way she does, she wants to encourage other people to dress the way *they* want to dress. Not to dress like she dresses. She said sometimes she'll look out her win-

Cyndi wearing one of her typically zany outfits.

Cyndi and friends. Even the very young have been influenced by her style.

dow and see people walking down the street who look just like her. She said she feels like she lives in a studio apartment full of mirrors."

Cyndi once told *People* about the problems of being a fashion trendsetter. "I *can* get carried away with the chains and the belts, the this and the that. By the time you finish, you go home and you're tired and you're so done up that you need a chain cutter to get undressed. So it's rough."

CYNDI VS. CAPTAIN LOU

When Cyndi lived in Ozone Park, she watched professional wrestling on TV with her grandfather. Professional wrestlers almost always wear funny outfits and have names like "The Executioner" or "The Junkyard Dog." In the crazy world of professional wrestling, you can't always tell if it's a put-on or not. It sure looks silly but those guys throw each other around so violently . . . who knows?

A true professional wrestling fan, Cyndi was thrilled when she met Captain Lou Albano on an airplane flight. Captain Lou manages such wrestlers as Greg "The Hammer" Valentine and the Wild Samoans. Cyndi was in awe of Lou. Little did she know that he would become one of her biggest fans!

"I met Cyndi Lauper some two years ago," Captain Lou relates. "I was on a plane coming back from Puerto Rico, and I talked to her. In fact, I went to her concert. And I saw 57,817 people in a full San Clemente stadium watching Cyndi Lauper. I was so amazed, I was so happy, I was so elated! I said, 'Captain! You've got to be a part of that!' I predict—I, Captain Lou Albano, Maker of Champions—predict that Cyndi Lauper will be the greatest entertainer of all time!"

Cyndi, needless to say, was equally impressed with Captain Lou. "The man's a genius," Cyndi told *No. 1*.

With Captain Lou Albano.

"He said to me, 'Cyndi, I am a Maker of Champions and I can make you one too.' And I said, 'Okay, Captain Lou!' He came up with the PEG Principle, which stands for Politeness, Etiquette, and Grooming. They're three very important principles in rock-'n'-roll, of course."

Cyndi was so taken with Captain Lou and his PEG Principle she put him in all three of her videos, although Captain Lou is only visible for a second or so in "Time after Time."

All of a sudden, a feud developed between them. Many feel it all began on "Piper's Pit," the talk show of "World Championship Wrestling." Captain Lou allegedly announced that *he* was Cyndi Lauper's manager, that *he* wrote all her songs, that *he* pulled Cyndi up from the gutter, and a number of other things too unbelievable to mention.

The next week, "Piper's Pit" became a battleground. Cyndi Lauper and Dave Wolff appeared in person to refute Lou Albano's wild claims. Lou and Cyndi found themselves in a shouting match that ended only when Cyndi had knocked over all the furniture on the set!

She issued a challenge to Lou Albano: she would put a wrestler of her own in the ring with the Fabulous Moolah, a woman wrestler managed by Captain Lou. She was the World Wrestling Federation women's champion, so Cyndi knew no ordinary wrestler could take her on. The wrestler Cyndi got was Wendi Richter. Wendi describes herself as "150 pounds of twisted steel and sex appeal." But would that be enough to mash the Moolah?

Well, as things turned out, it was enough. In a judge's decision, Wendi Richter was declared the winner and new World Wrestling Federation women's champion. Cyndi Lauper had become a "Maker of Champions" too!

It must be said that in the end, Captain Lou was a gentleman. In September 1984, Cyndi Lauper played a Concert at New York's Hudson River Pier. Captain Lou came on stage. Before thousands of Cyndi Lauper fans, Lou apologized for everything he had said.

"He was being a real *slug* for a while," Cyndi explained, "A real chauvinist slug. But you know, he's giving chauvinism a bad name. Oh yeah yeah, but he apologized. . . . He showed us the PEG Principle and we showed him the BAD Principle. He was Beaten, Annihilated, and Destroyed. He's not so bad, you know. He's really not so bad. He apologized. It's just that he has this calcium deposit in the medulla of his oblongata . . . He apologized to me, he apologized to all women for calling them slime and he apologized to my mother."

Is the feud between Cyndi and Captain Lou over with? For the moment anyway!

CYNDI ON THE TUBE

With hit songs on the radio and smash videos on MTV, were there any worlds left for Cyndi Lauper to conquer? Cyndi thought she'd give television a try.

When rock stars are on television, the results are often a disaster. Some rock-'n'-rollers aren't lively enough in front of the cameras. Other rock-'n'-rollers frighten their hosts that they'll do something crazy or outrageous on the air.

But people knew Cyndi Lauper was different. She was never at a loss for words and everyone loved her funny-sounding speaking voice. (Lots of people think Cyndi's voice is a put-on. Biff of Screaming Mimi's says otherwise: "She always had that same voice. Everybody always wants to know if that's for real. It *is* for real.")

Seeing Cyndi's wild outfits and wacky disposition, Johnny Carson decided to ask her to appear on his show. The "Tonight Show," starring Johnny Carson, is one of the longest-running television shows in the history of TV. Every celebrity imaginable has appeared on it. Comedians like Steve Martin and Joan Rivers owe much of their fame to appearances with Johnny Carson. Although he's a superb comedian himself, Carson is really just a quiet, conservative man from Nebraska.

In spite of all that, he loved Cyndi Lauper. She's been a

On Johnny Carson's "To-night Show."

With Rodney Dangerfield.

guest on the "Tonight Show" three times in six months during which Cyndi and her band have played "Girls Just Want to Have Fun," "Time after Time," "She Bop," and "All through the Night."

On her third trip to the show, Cyndi presented Johnny with her platinum record, saying, "Ever since I was on this show, a lot of good things happened." Don't be surprised if you see Cyndi Lauper on the "Tonight Show" again sometime soon.

Cyndi has appeared elsewhere on television, though. At the 1984 Grammy Awards she was teamed up with Rodney Dangerfield to present an award. Sometimes you see Cyndi Lauper with the oddest people. She's been seen on "Entertainment Tonight" playing miniature golf with Pee Wee Herman, the comedian. Maybe she had to find somebody with a funnier voice than hers.

Cyndi and her group played on "The New Show" which was cancelled only a few weeks later. Maybe if they'd let Cyndi sing *every* week, they'd still be on the air!

One of Cyndi's biggest television appearances was at the MTV Video Music Awards Show. At every awards ceremony, there are a few minutes at the beginning when someone has to read the rules and regulations. Since the reading of the rules is considered to be the most boring part of an awards show, guess who MTV chose to read their rules?

In front of a live, nationwide audience, Cyndi began:

> "As manager of the undisputed World Wrestling Federation women's champion, I, Cyndi Lauper, know about rules. Tonight I have decided, though, to read the rules in ancient Babylonian in honor of the late Hammurabi Maspweetin from the family of Yemyem. . . ."

That was the last thing that Cyndi said that anyone could understand. Even if she wasn't really speaking in

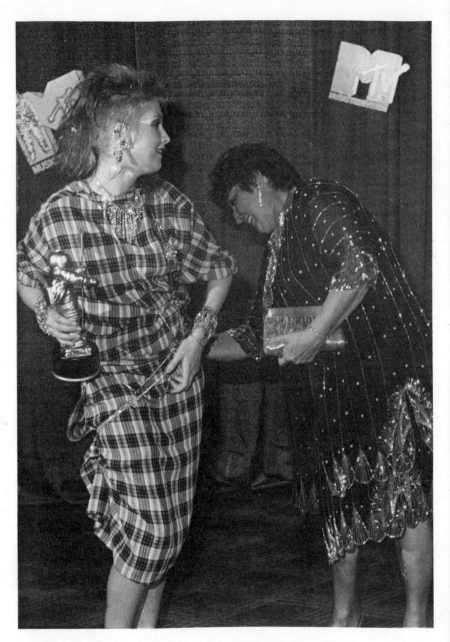

Cyndi with MTV award in hand and mom by her side.

Babylonian, Cyndi may as well have been. (The *real* rules to the MTV Awards were shown in English subtitles at the bottom of the TV screen.) By the time Cyndi was through, she may have set a world record for talking gibberish on national television!

Despite her clowning around, it was a tense night for Cyndi Lauper—she had been nominated for five different awards. In every category, it seemed, someone beat Cyndi to the award. People wondered if she would bring home even *one* MTV moonwalker statuette. Then, in the "Best Female Video" category, Cyndi heard her name called.

The award was for "Girls Just Want to Have Fun." Rushing up to the podium, she said breathlessly: "Boy, am I glad I won. Otherwise this tiara would've looked awfully stupid. Anyway, thank you very, very much!"

If anyone ever had any doubts about Cyndi, the MTV Awards would put them to rest. Cyndi had finally made it. She was a star.

A LOOK AT THE FUTURE

Cyndi Lauper became a #1 pop singer, a star of rock videos, a professional wrestling manager, and a television personality in the course of a *single year!*

Cyndi hasn't taken a moment to relax, however. In the fall of 1984, Cyndi and her band toured the country relentlessly. There's always another town that wants to hear her, and it seems like she tries to satisfy everyone.

Biff and Laura from Screaming Mimi's will be helping Cyndi on her new videos: live versions of "When You Were Mine" and "Money Changes Everything." After her tour ends, Cyndi expects to go back into the recording studio in 1985.

But how could all these things be happening to Cyndi Lauper?

Wasn't she the girl the other kids threw rocks at?

Wasn't she the girl who couldn't fit in at school?

Wasn't she the girl who they said couldn't sing?

Wasn't she the girl who had to declare herself legally bankrupt?

Well, Cyndi was that girl, but she isn't anymore. Those struggles are behind her now. She has challenged the odds and emerged as one of the most loved and respected rock-'n'-roll stars in the world.

Cyndi Lauper. She's more than just unusual.

She's unforgettable.

"She's more than just unusual. She's unforgettable!"

DISCOGRAPHY

ALBUMS

SHE'S SO UNUSUAL   **Portrait; 1983**
"Money Changes Everything" * "Girls Just
Want to Have Fun" * "When You Were Mine" *
"Time after Time" * "She Bop" * "All through
the Night" * "Witness" * "I'll Kiss You" * "He's
So Unusual" * "Yeah Yeah"*

BLUE ANGEL (featuring Cyndi Lauper) **Polydor; 1980**
"Maybe He'll Know" * "I Had a Love" *
"Fade" * "Anna Blue" * "Can't Blame Me" *
"Late" * "Cut Out" * "Take a Chance"* "Just
the Other Day" * "I'm Gonna Be Strong" *
"Lorraine" * "Everybody's Got an Angel"

SINGLES

"**GIRLS JUST WANT TO HAVE FUN**"   **Portrait; 1983**
  backed with "**RIGHT TRACK,**
  WRONG TRAIN"
"**TIME AFTER TIME**" backed with   **Portrait; 1984**
  "**I'LL KISS YOU**"
"**SHE BOP**" backed with "**WITNESS**" **Portrait; 1984**
"**ALL THROUGH THE NIGHT**" backed with **Portrait; 1984**
  "**WITNESS**"
"**I HAD A LOVE**" backed with "**TAKE** **Polydor; 1980**
  A CHANCE" (Blue Angel)

62